Let's Learn About... THE SKY

Teacher's Guide

Pre-Coding

K3

P Pearson

Pearson Education Limited
KAO Two, KAO Park, Harlow, Essex, CM17 9NA, England
and Associated Companies around the world.

© Pearson Education Limited 2020

TThe right of Luciana Pinheiro and Rhiannon Ball, to be identified as authors of this Work has been asserted by them in accordance with the Copyright, Designs and Patents Act 1988.

All rights reserved; no part of this publication may be reproduced, stored in a retrieval system, or transmitted in any form or by any means, electronic, mechanical, photocopying, recording, or otherwise without the prior written permission of the Publishers.

First published 2020

ISBN: 978-1-292-33444-8

Set in Mundo Sans
Printed in China (SWTC/01)

Acknowledgements
The publishers and author(s) would like to thank the following people and institutions for their feedback and comments during the development of the material: Marcos Mendonça, Leandra Dias, Viviane Kirmeliene, Rhiannon Ball, Simara H. Dal'Alba, Mônica Bicalho and GB Editorial. The publishers would also like to thank all the teachers who contributed to the develoment of Let's learn about...: Adriano de Paula Souza, Aline Ramos Teixeira Santo, Aline Vitor Rodrigues Pina Pereira, Ana Paula Gomez Montero, Anna Flávia Feitosa Passos, Camila Jarola, Celiane Junker Silva, Edegar França Junior, Fabiana Reis Yoshio, Fernanda de Souza Thomaz, Luana da Silva, Michael Iacovino Luidvinavicius, Munique Dias de Melo, Priscila Rossatti Duval Ferreira Neves, and Sandra Ferito.

Author Acknowledgements
Luciana Pinheiro and Rhiannon Ball

Image Credit(s):
Shutterstock.com: BeRad 16, GraphicsRF 28, Lemberg Vector studio 38, Martyshova Maria 18, Moloko88 26, MoRaven 16, Teguh Mujiono 12, vable 18

Illustration Acknowledgements
Illustrated by Filipe Laurentino and Silva Serviços de Educação.

Cover illustration © Filipe Laurentino

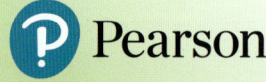

Contents

	Table of Contents	4
	Presentation	6
U1	Who do you like to play with?	8
U2	What parts of your body help you feel?	12
U3	Why is your family important to you?	16
U4	What happens to your body when you are hot or cold?	20
U5	Why is it important to take care of our planet?	24
U6	How can you stay healthy?	28
U7	How can you take care of animals?	32
U8	What is your favorite place in town?	36

Table of Contents — Pre-Coding

UNIT	LESSON 1	LESSON 2
Unit 1 Who do you like to play with? page 08	• Identify and complete a pattern • Practice using vocabulary related to height, hair color, and eye color **Pre-Coding Skills:** • Patterns	• Complete a symmetrical drawing • Practice using vocabulary related to feelings **Pre-Coding Skills:** • Symmetry
Unit 2 What parts of your body help you feel? page 12	• Find the bugs in a sequence • Practice using vocabulary related to body parts and the senses **Pre-Coding Skills:** • Debugging	• Put numbers in the correct order • Practice using vocabulary related to musical instruments and numbers 1 to 50 **Pre-Coding Skills:** • Sequence
Unit 3 Why is your family Important to you? page 16	• Decompose numbers 1 to 10 • Practice using the concept and language related to measuring weight **Pre-Coding Skills:** • Decomposition	• Recognize that the causes and consequences of actions • Practice using vocabulary related to family members **Pre-Coding Skills:** • Branching (*If-Then*)
Unit 4 What happens to your body when you are hot or cold? page 20	• Recognize a mistake in a pattern • Practice using the concept and language related to measuring weight **Pre-Coding Skills:** • Debugging	• Count variables through a game • Practice using vocabulary related to clothes **Pre-Coding Skills:** • Variables

UNIT	LESSON 1	LESSON 2
Unit 5 Why is it important to take care of our planet? page 24	• Create a sequence • Practice using vocabulary related to helping the environment **Pre-Coding Skills:** • Sequence	• Recognize a pattern • Practice using vocabulary related to animals in different habitats **Pre-Coding Skills:** • Patterns
Unit 6 How can you stay healthy? page 28	• Match an algorithm to a maze • Practice using vocabulary related to healthy habits **Pre-Coding Skills:** • Sequences	• Break down a picture into smaller part • Practice using vocabulary related to food **Pre-Coding Skills:** • Decomposition
Unit 7 How can you take care of animals? page 32	• Recognize and follow a numbers sequence • Practice talking about wild animals **Pre-Coding Skills:** • Sequences	• Recognize that the causes and consequences of actions • Practice reading the time on the hour **Pre-Coding Skills:** • Branching (If-Then)
Unit 8 What is your favorite place in town? page 36	• Recognize mistakes in a picture • Talk about what people do and where they do it **Pre-Coding Skills:** • Debugging • Logical thinking	• Identify how many times something needs to be done to get a result • Talk about what people do and where they do it **Pre-Coding Skills:** • Looping

Presentation

Let's Learn About... is a bilingual program which aims to develop a wide variety of skills and knowledge of different subjects. To this end, several additional components ensure that students work on creative learning, pre-coding, STEAM lessons, personal, social, and emotional development, and much more. Teachers can find a complete mapping of the components online and suggested weekly planning to help them make the most of the interdisciplinary approach. All of the components in the program provide students with the opportunity to build a solid foundation and prepare themselves for the challenges ahead. The lessons help children explore and learn more about the world around them. The *Pre-Coding Project Book* helps students explore and learn more about the *digital world* around them.

What is coding?

Coding is a programming language that is used to get a computer to behave how you want it to. It is present in everyday life, in all of the machines and technology that we use on a daily basis. Think about when you wash clothes: how does a modern washing machine know when to start? When you press "go" on the digital screen, a pre-programmed code tells the washing machine that it needs to start the wash cycle.

Learning principles behind Pre-Coding in *Let's Learn about...*

Children of preschool and kindergarten age in the 21st Century are living in a rapidly changing world that is dominated by continuously evolving technology. These children are digital natives, which means that they don't know a life without smartphones, the Internet, computers, etc. Most will be used to handling and playing with technology, so they are already ready to start working on something that can be challenging and even intimidating for many adults: coding.

Computer programmers need to have well-developed problem-solving, logical thinking, and decision-making skills to program codes and find problems in codes when a computer isn't behaving the way it should. Therefore, the *Pre-Coding* component in **Let's Learn About...** aims to help students develop these important skills. We want students to start thinking like computer programmers, and this is best done through play. That's why the *Pre-Coding* component is completely screenless.

Students will start developing skills through fun games, drawing, coloring and sticker activities, and hands-on activities, working both individually and with their classmates. All of these activities lay an important foundation for students to start coding with real computers when they move on in their learning journey.

What's in a Pre-Coding lesson?

Pre-Coding lessons follow similar routines to the ones that students develop in all the **Let's Learn About...** components, including the visual schedule, attention-getters, and *hello* and *goodbye* songs and routines.

Each lesson works on a coding skill, with students taking part in a teacher-led activity before putting this into practice through a hands-on activity in the Project Book. Lessons are topic-based according to the core Student's Book, so students have the opportunity to practice their language skills further.

Although the concept is screen-free, you may like to spark students' interest and imagination by telling them that they are computer programmers in these classes, and their job is to make things happen and fix problems, just like real computer programmers! A fun computer character appears occasionally throughout the Project Book to reinforce this activity and to add a level of familiarity, which is important for students of this age.

Pre-Coding Glossary

The *Pre-Coding* component works on the following coding skills and concepts. These are explained throughout the Teacher's Guide. From K2 onwards, you may like to start using these words with your students, but avoid giving long, complex explanations or expecting them to understand the meaning. Simply use the word as you are demonstrating or participating in an activity.

Algorithm: Refers to a sequence of instructions that tells a computer to do something.
Decomposition: Refers to breaking down a problem into smaller parts that are easier to deal with.
Debugging: Refers to identifying mistakes in a code (or pattern). In coding, mistakes in patterns are called "bugs" and they stop the computer doing what it should do.
If-Then: Refers to a concept of action and consequence, e.g. *if* this is true, *then* this will happen/is true. In coding, computers make choices depending on whether something is true or not. In this activity, students jump to the correct side of the rope according to if it's correct or not.
Looping: Refers to an algorithm (set of instructions) that repeats a certain number until a specific result is achieved.
Pattern: When there is a problem with a program or app the coders look for patterns that they have not seen before. If they find these patterns, they will know what is wrong and they will be able to fix it.
Symmetry: Refers to a shape looking exactly the same as another one when you move it in the same way.
Sequencing: Refers to organizing objects, numbers, etc. in a specific order. In coding, sequences tell the computer the order in which they need to do things.
Variables: Refers to where information is stored, and it is a factor that can change.

Components

For teachers
- Pre-Coding Teacher's Guide
- Audio library with songs available at Pearson English Portal

For students
- Pre-Coding Project Book with stickers

Presentation 7

Unit 1 Who do you like to play with?

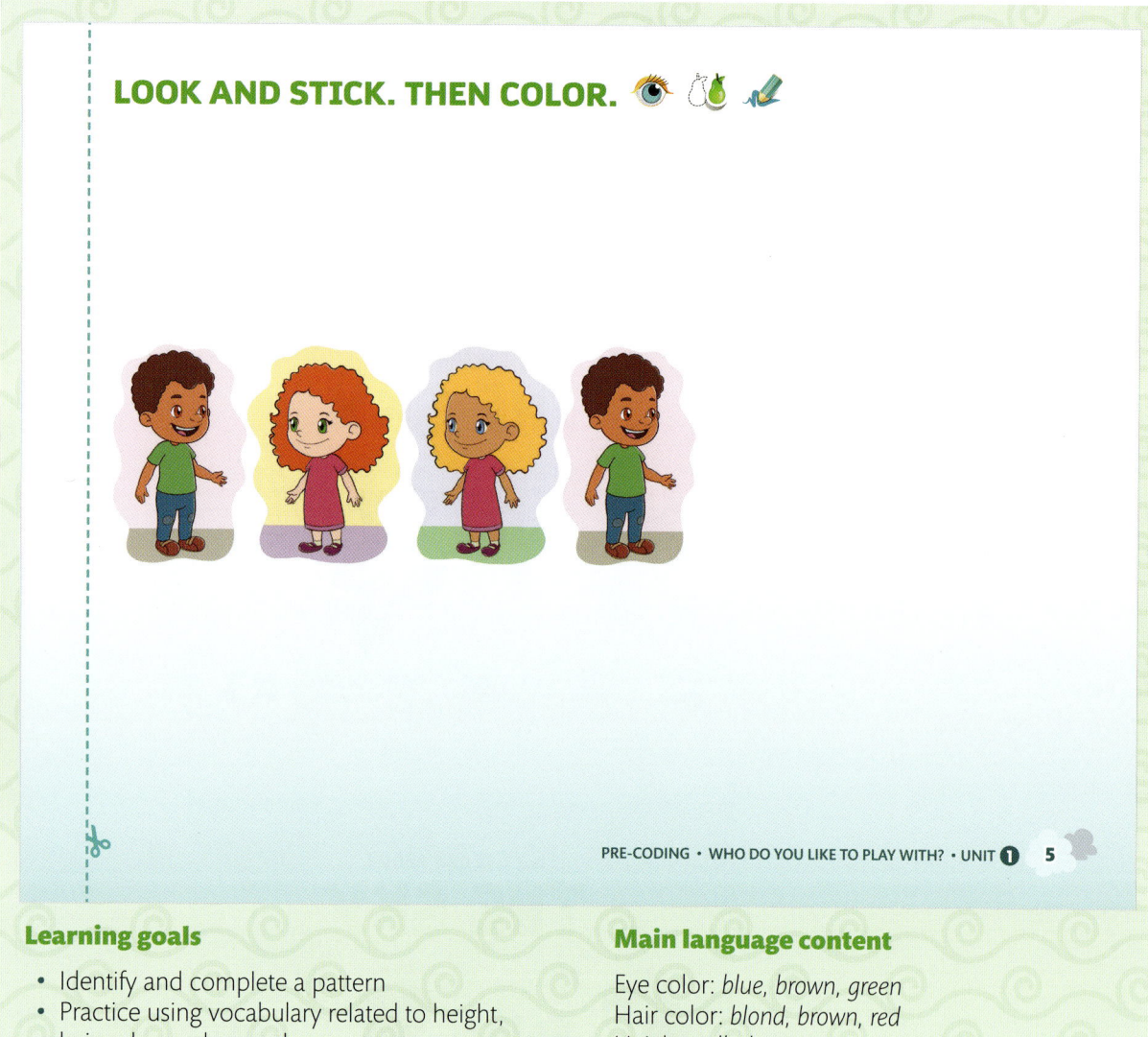

Learning goals
- Identify and complete a pattern
- Practice using vocabulary related to height, hair color, and eye color

Pre-coding skill
- Pattern

Main language content
Eye color: *blue, brown, green*
Hair color: *blond, brown, red*
Height: *tall, short*
I am tall.
I have brown hair and blue eyes.

OPENING

Circle time

Materials and preparation
- Audio library – songs
- Puppet

Say *hello* to students and encourage them to greet you back. Introduce the puppet to those who haven't met it or ask for students' help to do so.
Sing the *Hello song* (track 2) and have them sing, mime, and dance.
Have students sit in a circle. Choose a name for the puppet together with the class if this hasn't already been done in another class.
Teach students the opening attention-getter:
T: *Let's take this road!*
S: *It's time to code!*
or
T: *Turn on your fun mode because it's time to...*
S: *Code!*
Explain to students that whenever you use an attention-getter, they should stop talking and look at you.

> **Note to teachers**
> You can also teach/review the attention-getter *All set? You bet!*

What's the schedule for today's lesson?

Materials and preparation
- Visual schedule pictures

Show each picture and then separate the ones that show the activities of today's class. Have a volunteer place the activities in the middle of the circle.

Note to teachers
Although students won't be using screens during these activities, a "computer" character will appear to help them associate the basic function of coding, which is to get a computer to achieve a specific task. They will develop pre-coding skills in all lessons; however, in lessons with the computer character, you can be more explicit in explaining that they are "coders" and they need to help the computer do something.

ACTIVE LEARNING

Identifying hair and eye color

Materials and preparation
- Magazine cutouts or printouts of people with different hair and eye colors (blue, brown, green; blond, brown, red)

Show students the magazine cutouts/printouts and explore the pictures with them. Point to the hair and eyes, ask, *What color are they?* and encourage students to say *blond hair/green eyes*. Have students sit in a circle, and spread the pictures in the middle. Invite students to categorize and sort the pictures. Then take one picture from each category and arrange the pictures on the floor in a pattern. Invite students to continue adding pictures to complete the pattern.

Note to teachers
Allowing students to choose how to categorize the pictures helps them develop autonomy.

Look and stick. Then color.
Materials and preparation
- Crayons or colored pencils
- Project Book page 5

Help students open their Project Books to page 5. Have them observe the page. Help them notice that the children are different heights. Say, *Point to someone who's tall*. Then say, *Point to someone who's short*. Encourage them to notice the pattern and think about what comes next. Help students turn to the stickers page at the back of the book, peel off the stickers, and stick them in the correct place to complete the pattern. Help them with the stickers as needed.

Note to teachers
This activity helps students practice spotting patterns. When there is a problem with a program or app the coders look for patterns that they have not seen before. If they find these patterns they will know what is wrong and they will be able to fix it.

Now students are going to complete the pattern according to eye and hair color. Divide students into pairs. Together, they notice the pattern and color the stickers to complete it. At the end of the activity, invite more confident students to describe the pictures in the pattern.

Note to teachers
You can extend this activity by challenging students to make the pattern in person! Have students identify same hair and eye colors in their classmates and form a line in a pattern similar to the one shown in the Project Book.

DIFFERENTIATED INSTRUCTION

BELOW LEVEL
Look and stick. Then color.

Go over the patterns with students, pointing to each picture at a time, and help them identify what comes next.

ABOVE LEVEL
Look and stick. Then color.

Students draw and color another person to continue the pattern.

CLOSING

Create a pattern.
Sing the *Goodbye song*.

Materials and preparation
- Audio library – songs

Students stand up and organize themselves so that they make a pattern according to their height, e.g. a tall student, a short student, a tall student, etc. If appropriate, you could take a picture of them to display on the classroom board and label it accordingly.
Sing the *Goodbye song* (track 3) and invite students to sing along. Say *goodbye* to them and have them say *goodbye* back to you.

Learning goals
- Complete a symmetrical drawing
- Practice using words for feelings

Pre-coding skill
- Symmetry

Main language content

Feelings: *happy, sad, scared, surprised*
Shapes: *circle, hexagon, rhombus, square, trapezoid, triangle*
How are you? I'm happy.

OPENING

Circle time

Materials and preparation
- Puppet
- Visual schedule pictures

Show the puppet to students and have them greet it with *hello* or *hi*. Remind students of the attention-getter and practice it with them:
T: *Let's take this road!*
S: *It's time to code!*
or
T: *Turn on your fun mode because it's time to...*
S: *Code!*
Show students the visual schedule pictures. Ask for volunteers to help you turn them over. Encourage the whole class to say what each picture shows. Ask students to help you select the pictures that show today's schedule as you tell them what they are going to do today.

> **Note to teachers**
> Remind students that they should be quiet and pay attention when you use the attention-getter.

Play *Mirror me*

Materials and preparation
- A mirror (optional)

Divide students into pairs, one standing in front of each other. Explain that you are going to play a game where students will be mirroring each other. Ask one of the students of the pair to start making motions and have the other student mirror those motions. After a while, ask students to switch roles.

Note to teachers
This activity introduces the idea of symmetry. If possible, reinforce the idea of mirrors and symmetry by passing around a mirror for students to look at their reflection, or talking to them about what they see in a mirror, e.g. *What happens if you touch your face when you look in a mirror?* (your reflection touches your face, too!)

ACTIVE LEARNING

Symmetry
Materials and preparation
- Cutouts of shapes or blocks
- Masking tape

Divide students into pairs and have them sit together at a table. Stick some masking tape between them vertically and give them blocks or shape cutouts. Instruct one of the students to make a pattern on their side of the masking tape, making sure one part of the pattern touches the masking tape/vertical line. Then the other student copies the pattern on their side of the tape. Walk around students asking them to describe their patterns.

Note to teachers
Students may struggle to remember shapes and colors, so you can review these before the activity.

Draw and color.
Materials and preparation
- Crayons
- Pencils
- Project Book page 7

Help students open their Project Books to page 7. Ask, *What can you see? What is missing?* Encourage them to think about how to complete the missing parts. Students draw the faces using the grids to help them. Then they can color the pictures.

Note to teachers
This activity features a computer character, which reinforces the idea of learning skills that are useful for coding. Whenever students do activities featuring the computer character, tell them that they are "coders" and they are telling the computer what to do. In this activity, the "coders" are telling the computer to make different facial expressions by completing the drawing.

Symmetrical face
Materials and preparation
- Play dough
- Project Book page 7

Once students have finished coloring the pictures in their Project Books, ask them to identify the feelings. Check if they can name other feelings. As you practice saying the words with them, ask them to make funny faces showing the feeling. Then give out play dough for students to make faces. Invite them to show their faces to a classmate and say what feeling the face shows. Encourage them to notice if the faces are symmetrical.

DIFFERENTIATED INSTRUCTION

BELOW LEVEL
Draw and color.

Go over the grids with students and point to the face parts. Explain what each block represents and show students how to count the blocks on the grid to mirror the face.

ABOVE LEVEL
Draw and color.

Invite students to look around the classroom and point out where they can see symmetry in the items around them. Encourage them to name the items they already know. Ask, *How are they symmetrical?*

CLOSING

Sort out the pictures.
Sing the *Goodbye song*.

Materials and preparation
- Audio library – songs
- Several pictures of happy, sad, scared, and surprised people of different ethnic groups

Have students sit in a circle. Spread the pictures in the middle of the circle and ask students to sort out the pictures according to the feelings (happy, sad, scared, and surprised).
Sing the *Goodbye song* (track 3) and invite students to sing along. Say *goodbye* to them and have them say *goodbye* back to you.

Unit 1

Unit 2 What parts of your body help you feel?

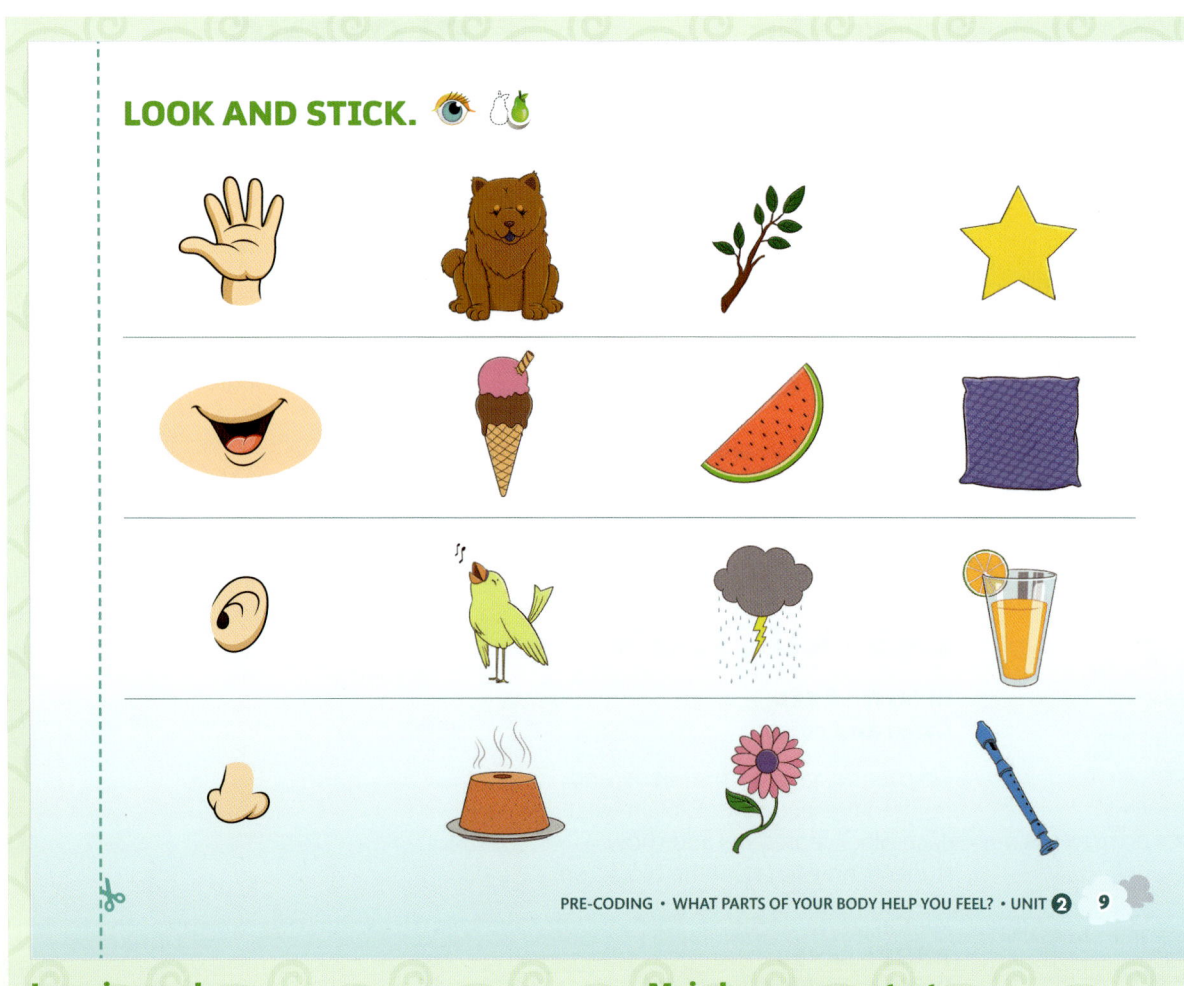

OPENING

Circle time

Materials and preparation
- Audio library – songs
- Puppet
- Visual schedule pictures

Show the puppet to students and have them greet it with *hello* or *hi*. Sing the *Hello song* (track 2) and have them sing, mime, and dance. Remind students of the attention-getter and practice it with them:
T: *Let's take this road!*
S: *It's time to code!*
or
T: *Turn on your fun mode because it's time to…*
S: *Code!*
Have students sit in a circle. Show them the visual schedule pictures. Choose a class helper of the day and have them order the pictures of the activities as they are mentioned.

> **Note to teachers**
> You can also teach/review the attention-getter *All set? You bet!*

Sing *Head, shoulders, knees, and toes*.

Materials and preparation
- Audio library – songs

Sing *Heads, shoulders, knees, and toes* (track 13). Encourage students to stand up, sing the song, and do the actions. Divide students into pairs. One student sings the song while the other touches the correct body part. Then they switch roles. Depending on how confident your students are, you can do this with or without the music.

Learning goals
- Find the bugs in a sequence
- Practice using words for body parts and the senses

Pre-coding skill
- Debugging

Main language content
Parts of the body: *hands, head, knees, shoulders, toes*
Parts of the face: *ears, eyes, nose, mouth*
Senses: *hear, see, smell, taste, touch*
What do we do with this part of the body?

ACTIVE LEARNING

Our senses

Materials and preparation

- Audio library – songs

Play and sing the chorus of the *Heads, shoulder, knees, and toes* song only (*eyes, ears, mouth, and nose*). Then point to the parts of the face and ask, *What do we do with this part of the body?* Encourage students to name the senses. Call out the names of the senses, students have to point to the correct body part. They can act out the sense, e.g. pretending to taste an ice cream, listen to music, etc.

Look and stick.

Materials and preparation

- Project Book page 9

Help students open their Project Books to page 9. Point to the hand and ask students, *What do we do with this part of the body?* Show them the pictures next to the body part and ask, *What's wrong?* to help them identify which picture doesn't match the sense (touch). Point to each picture until students identify the "bug". Repeat the procedure for the other body parts/senses. Students turn to the stickers page at the back of the book, peel off the bug stickers, and then stick the bug on the incorrect image. Help them with the stickers as needed.

> **Note to teachers**
> In this activity, students have to identify mistakes in a pattern. In coding, mistakes in patterns are called *bugs* and they stop the computer doing what it should do.

DIFFERENTIATED INSTRUCTION

BELOW LEVEL
Look and stick.

Have students do the activity in pairs and help them identify the "bug" by pointing to each picture.

ABOVE LEVEL
Look and stick.

Materials and preparation

- Crayons or colored pencils
- Sheets of paper

On a separate sheet of paper, students can draw another pattern for a sense/body part.

CLOSING

Play *Who is it?* Sing the *Goodbye song*.

Materials and preparation

- Audio library – songs
- Blindfold

Choose a student to wear the blindfold and have them stand still. Bring one of their classmates in front of them and have them touch the classmate's face. Ask if they can guess who they are just by touching their face and hair.
Sing the *Goodbye song* (track 3) and invite students to sing along. Say *goodbye* to them and have them say *goodbye* back to you.

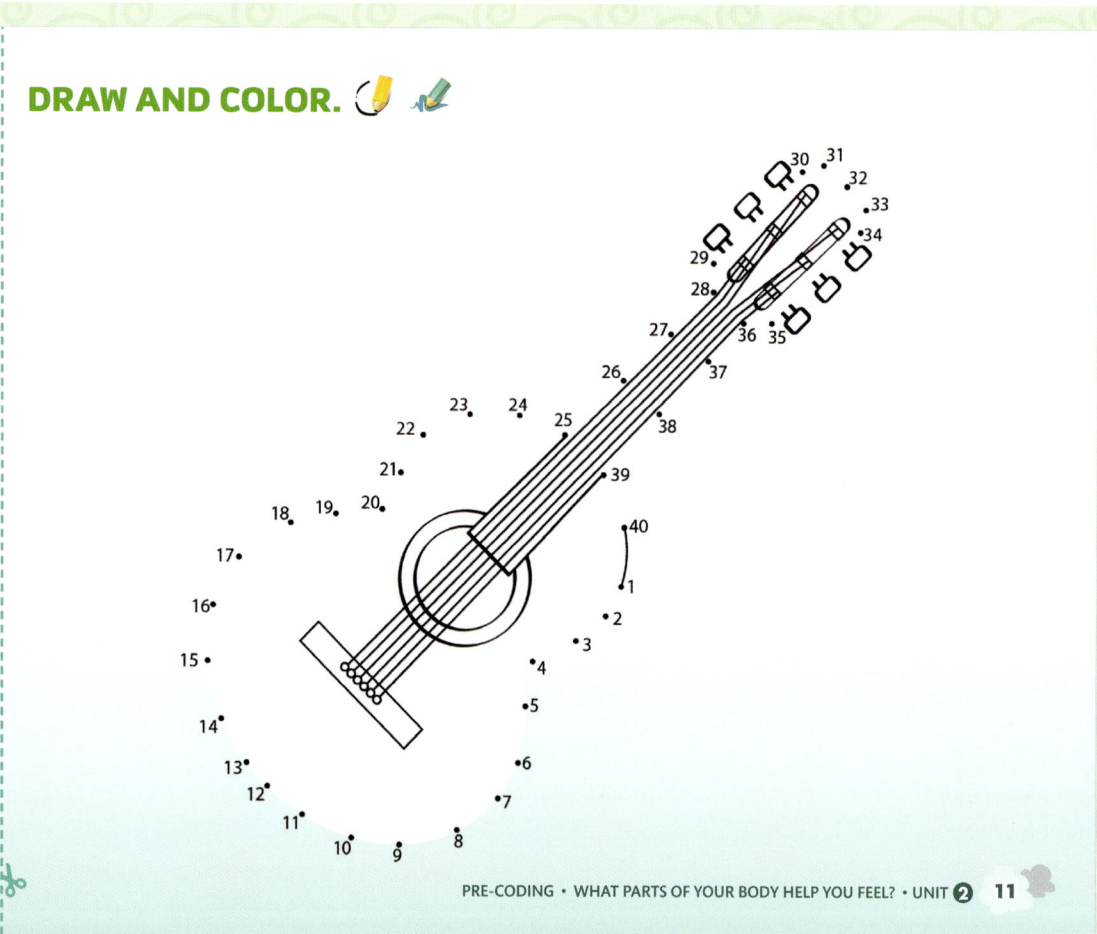

Learning goals
- Put numbers in the correct order
- Practice using words for musical instruments and numbers 1 to 40

Pre-coding skill
- Sequence

Main language content

Musical instruments: *cymbals, drum, guitar, tambourine, triangle*
Numbers: *1-40*
What am I doing? I'm playing a (violin).

OPENING

Circle time

Materials and preparation
- Puppet
- Visual schedule pictures (hide them around the classroom)

Show the puppet to students and have them greet it with *hello* or *hi*. Remind students of the attention-getter and practice it with them:
T: *Let's take this road!*
S: *It's time to code!*
or
T: *Turn on your fun mode because it's time to…*
S: *Code!*
Hide the visual schedule pictures that refer to today's activities. Tell students to look for them around the classroom. As they find a picture, tell them to hand it to you. Then talk to students about each of the moments of the class.

> **Note to teachers**
> Remind students that they should be quiet and pay attention when you use the attention-getter.

Class orchestra

Mime playing a musical instrument and ask students, *What am I doing?* Invite them to stand up and mime playing different musical instruments. Encourage them to say *I'm playing the (guitar)*. Ask the other students to imagine what the music their classmate is playing sounds like. Encourage them to make the sound using their body (e.g. their mouth, hands, feet, etc.)

ACTIVE LEARNING

Count to 40!

Materials and preparation
- A jar or a translucent bag filled with forty buttons

Gather students in a circle and pass the jar/bag around the circle. Invite students to guess how many buttons are in the jar/bag. Then take the buttons out one by one and count them together with students.

> **Note to teachers**
> If you have a small class, you can write students' guesses on the board to check later.

Draw and color.

Materials and preparation
- Crayons
- Pencils
- Project Book page 11

Help students open their Project Books to page 11. Ask students what instrument they think it is. Students use a pencil to join the dots and complete the drawing. When they have finished, check their guesses and ask them to color the picture. Have them repeat, *It's a guitar!*

> **Note to teachers**
> Encourage students to count the numbers aloud as they join the dots. This activity reinforces forward sequencing skills, which are important in coding because they tell the computer the order in which they need to do things.

My guitar

Materials and preparation
- Colored rectangles cutouts (one per student)
- Glue
- Paper plates
- String (three short pieces per student)

Hand out the materials and ask students to guess what you are going to make. Tell them that they are going to make a guitar! Give students the instructions in this order, *Glue the rectangle to the plate, draw a circle in the middle, stick the strings to the rectangle.* Make sure they follow the order to practice their sequencing skills. If you have time, students can color the paper plates.

DIFFERENTIATED INSTRUCTION

BELOW LEVEL
Draw and color.

Sit with students and help them count the numbers as they draw the line. If you have a large class, you can organize students into pairs (above-level with below-level students) and encourage them to help each other.

ABOVE LEVEL
Draw and color.

Materials and preparation
- Crayons or colored pencils
- Sheets of paper

Hand out a sheet of paper to students and encourage them to draw more musical instruments.

CLOSING

Play the guitar. Sing the *Goodbye song.*

Materials and preparation
- Audio library – songs
- Students' paper plate guitars

Invite students to stand up and pretend to play their paper plate guitar.
Play the *Goodbye song* (track 3) and invite students to sing along. Say *goodbye* to them and have them say *goodbye* back to you.

Unit 3 Why is your family important to you?

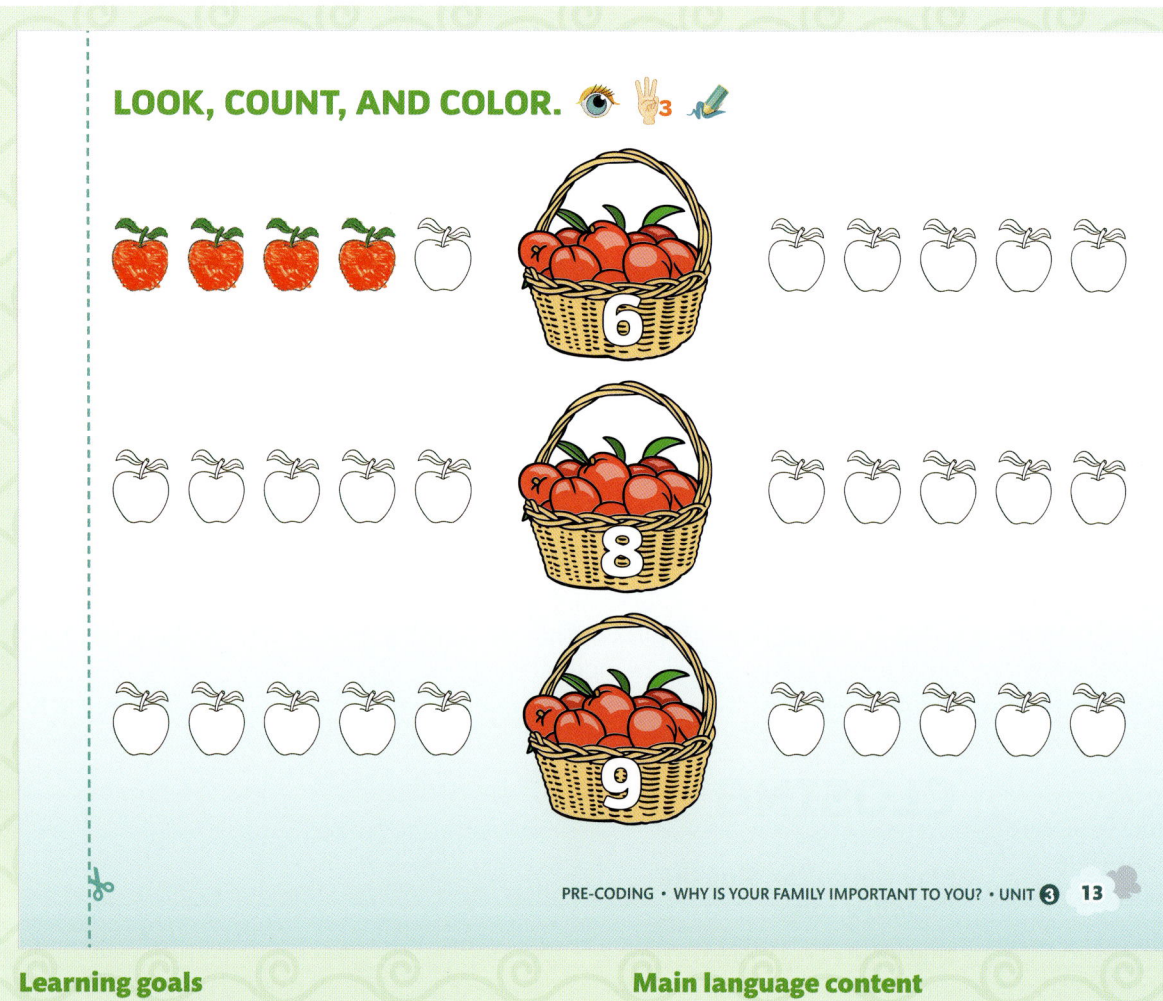

Learning goals
- Decompose numbers 1 to 10
- Practice using the concept and language related to measuring weight

Pre-coding skill
- Decomposition

Main language content
Numbers: 1-10
Vocabulary associated with weight: *heavy, heavier, less, light, lighter, more*
What is heavier?
This is heavier. This is lighter.

OPENING

Circle time

Materials and preparation
- Audio library – songs
- Puppet
- Visual schedule pictures

Show the puppet to students and have them greet it with *hello* or *hi*. Sing the *Hello song* (track 2) and have them sing, mime, and dance. Remind students of the attention-getter and practice it with them:
T: *Let's take this road!*
S: *It's time to code!*
or
T: *Turn on your fun mode because it's time to…*
S: *Code!*
Have students sit in a circle. Show each visual schedule picture and then separate the ones that show the activities of today's class. Have a volunteer place the activities in the middle of the circle.

> **Note to teachers**
> You can also teach/review the attention-getter *All set? You bet!*

Sing 1, 2, 3, 4, 5 once I caught a fish alive.

Materials and preparation
- Audio library – songs

Play the song *1, 2, 3, 4, 5 once I caught a fish alive* (track 14) and encourage students to sing along while counting with their fingers. Pause the song after a number is mentioned (e. g. 1, 2…) and encourage students to keep on singing/counting without the music.

ACTIVE LEARNING

Heavy or light?

Materials and preparation

- A variety of heavy and light objects, e.g. a feather, a pen, a thick book, etc.

Gather students in a circle. Put the heavy and light objects in the middle of the circle. Point to the objects and ask, *Is this light? Is this heavy?* Invite students to guess and then pick up the objects to confirm their weight. Then pick two objects and have students compare them. Ask, *Is this heavier? Is this lighter?* and encourage students to identify the heaviest and the lightest ones.

Make the bucket lighter

Materials and preparation

- 3 small buckets
- Several stones

Fill up a bucket with stones and invite students to try to (carefully) pick it up. Help them notice that it's heavy. Tell students that they need to take the stones to the yard, but it's too heavy to carry them. Ask them how they could take the stones to the yard. Encourage them to share their ideas. Explain that you are going to divide the stones into two buckets. Count the stones out of the bucket with students, and then ask them to help you divide them between the two buckets. For example, if there are 10 stones in the bucket, they can put four stones in one bucket and six stones in the other bucket. Try different combinations in the bucket to show students how the number of stones can be broken down into smaller numbers.

Look, count, and color.

Materials and preparation

- Crayons or colored pencils
- Project Book page 13

Help students open their Project Books to page 13. Ask them to read the numbers in the baskets of apples. Tell them that the baskets are too heavy, so they are going to divide the weight in them. Help them count how many apples are colored on the right side and ask, *How many apples do we need to color on the other side?* Students count and color to make up the number in the basket. Then they decide how to separate the apples in the other lines.

Note to teachers

This activity practices decomposition because students break down a large number into smaller ones. In coding, this process is used to break down a problem into smaller parts that are easier to deal with.

DIFFERENTIATED INSTRUCTION

BELOW LEVEL
Look, count, and color.

Materials and preparation

- Beans

Give students ten beans. They count out the number of beans according to the number on the bucket and place them in the middle of the page. Then place some beans on each side of the page to work out how to break down the number before they color the apples.

ABOVE LEVEL
Look, count, and color.

Materials and preparation

- Crayons or colored pencils
- Sheets of paper

On a separate sheet of paper, students can draw another basket of apples and divide them into two numbers.

CLOSING

Add up the blocks. Sing the *Goodbye song*.

Materials and preparation

- Audio library – songs
- Blocks

Sit with students in a circle and spread the blocks in the middle of the circle. Experiment adding up the blocks in different combinations. For example, show them five blocks, then show three blocks plus two blocks. Have them count and see how it is possible to decompose the number of blocks.

Note to teachers

If you think it is appropriate, write a simple sum on the board (e.g. ___ + ___ = 3). Have students think about different ways to make three. They can use the blocks to help them decompose the number.

Sing the *Goodbye song* (track 3) and invite students to sing along. Say *goodbye* to them and have them say *goodbye* back to you.

PLAY THE GAME!

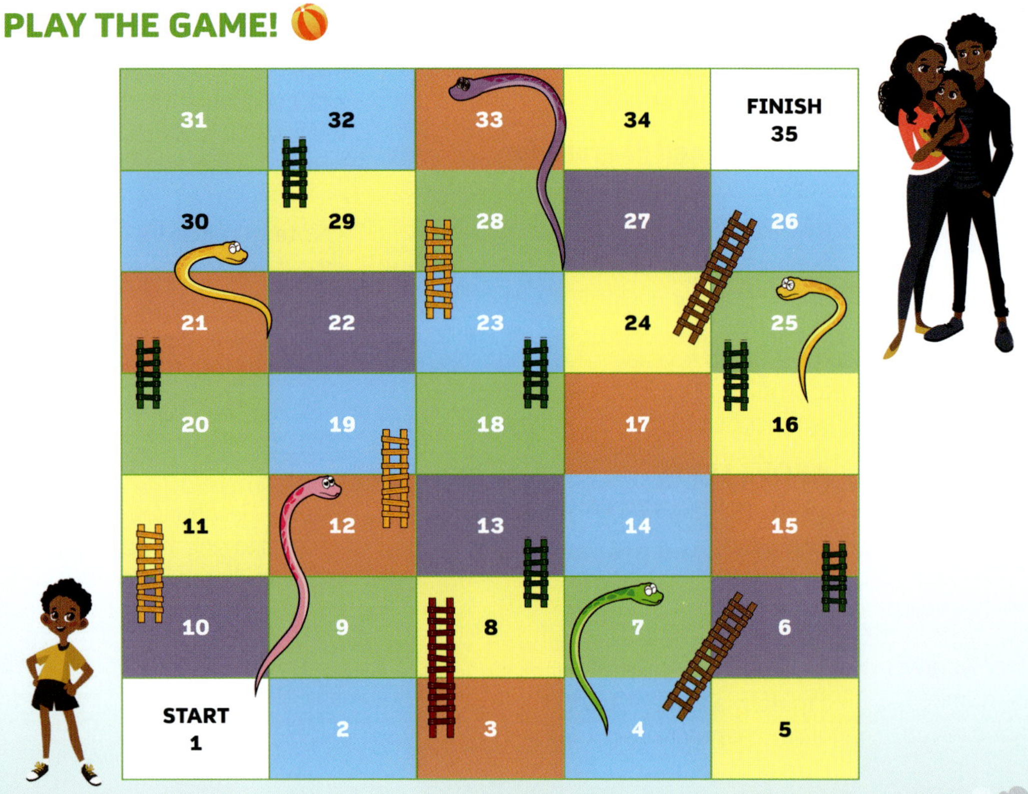

[Snakes and Ladders board game, numbered 1 (START) to 35 (FINISH)]

PRE-CODING • WHY IS YOUR FAMILY IMPORTANT TO YOU? • UNIT 3   15

Learning goals
- Recognize causes and consequences of actions
- Practice using words for family members

Pre-coding skill
- If-Then

Main language content
Family members: *aunt, brother, cousin, dad, grandma, grandpa, mom, sister, uncle*

OPENING

Circle time

Materials and preparation
- Puppet
- Visual schedule pictures

Show the puppet to students and have them greet it with *hello* or *hi*. Remind students of the attention-getter and practice it with them:
T: *Let's take this road!*
S: *It's time to code!*
or
T: *Turn on your fun mode because it's time to…*
S: *Code!*
Show students the visual schedule pictures. Ask for volunteers to help you turn them over. Encourage the whole class to say what each picture shows. Ask students to help you select the pictures that show today's schedule as you tell them what they are going to do today.

> **Note to teachers**
> Remind students that they should be quiet and pay attention when you use the attention-getter.

Family members
- A long rope
- Flashcards: *aunt, brother, cousin, dad, grandma, grandpa, mom, sister, uncle*

Place the rope on the floor in the middle of the classroom and tell students that one side is "yes" and the other side is "no". Hold up the flashcards one by one and say the name for the family member — sometimes you should say the correct word for the flashcard and sometimes say the incorrect word. Students move to the "yes" or "no" side of the rope according to whether you say the correct word or not.

18 Pre-coding

Note to teachers

All of the activities in this lesson allow students to practice the concept of "if-then" statements. In coding, computers make choices depending on whether something is true or not. In this activity, students jump to the correct side of the rope according to if it's correct or not.

ACTIVE LEARNING

Family commands
- Flashcards: *dad, grandpa, mom, sister*

Have students sit in a circle. Show the flashcards and ask, *Who's this?* Elicit the answer. Encourage them to say other family members that they know. Then ask them to think about what the family members on the flashcards usually say or do and help them assign an activity to each family member, e.g. *dad — pretend to cook dinner, mom — pretend to drive the car, baby sister — pretend to cry, grandpa — pretend to watch TV.* Tell students that as you show each flashcard, they need to do the action. Show the flashcards at random for students to do the action.

Play the game!
Materials and preparation
- Counters (or any small object that can be used as a counter)
- Dice (one per pair of students)
- Project Book page 15

Help students open their Project Books to page 15. Show the board game to students and tell them that they need to help the boy get to his family by playing the game. Ask students to explain the rules to you. Ask, *What happens if you get to a snake?* (You slide down it) *What happens if you roll a six on the die?* (You move six spaces along the board) *What happens if you get to the bottom of a ladder?* (You move up to the top of that ladder.) Pair students up, give them the dice and counters, and have them play the game. As students roll the dice, encourage them to say the number they get. If students finish quickly, they can switch pairs and play again.

Note to teachers

Discussing the rules as suggested reinforces the concept of "if-then" as students associate actions with consequences.

DIFFERENTIATED INSTRUCTION

BELOW LEVEL
Play the game!

Students can play in small groups so that they can receive instruction from their classmates when they get stuck.

ABOVE LEVEL
Play the game!

Have students talk about the route they took in the game by pointing with their finger. Encourage them to say *left, right, up, down*.

CLOSING

Play *Simon says*. Sing the *Goodbye song*.

Materials and preparation
- Audio library – songs

Play *Simon says* with students. Make sure they understand that if you say *Simon says*, they should do as you say and if not, they don't do anything.
Sing the *Goodbye song* (track 3) and invite students to sing along. Say *goodbye* to them and have them say *goodbye* back to you.

Unit 4 What happens to your body when you are hot or cold?

LOOK AND STICK. DRAW.

PRE-CODING • WHAT HAPPENS TO YOUR BODY WHEN YOU ARE HOT OR COLD? • UNIT 4   17

Learning goals
- Recognize a mistake in a pattern
- Practice using words related to weather

Pre-coding skill
- Debugging

Main language content
Clothes: *raincoat, rubber boots, shorts, skirt, sunglasses, T-shirt, umbrella*
Weather: *cold, hot, rainy*

OPENING

Circle time

Materials and preparation
- Audio library – songs
- Puppet
- Visual schedule pictures

Show the puppet to students and have them greet it with *hello* or *hi*. Sing the Hello song (track 2) and have them sing, mime, and dance. Remind students of the attention-getter and practice it with them:
T: *Let's take this road!*
S: *It's time to code!*
or
T: *Turn on your fun mode because it's time to…*
S: *Code!*
Have students sit in a circle. Show them the visual schedule pictures. Ask for volunteers to help you turn them over. Encourage the whole class to say what each picture shows. Choose a class helper of the day and have them order the pictures of the activities as they are mentioned.

> **Note to teachers**
> You can also teach/review the attention-getter *All set? You bet!*

Sing *Mama's taking us to the beach tomorrow.*

Materials and preparation
- Audio library – songs

Sing *Mama's taking us to the beach tomorrow* (track 7) and encourage students to sing along and do the gestures. Pause the song occasionally and encourage students to keep on singing without the music.

20 Pre-coding

ACTIVE LEARNING

The island

Divide students into small groups. Explain that each group is an island and each island has different weather. In their groups, students act out their island weather. The other students have to guess the weather. Then gather students in a circle and have them discuss what clothes they would need to wear on each island, according to the weather.

Hot or cold?

Materials and preparation

- Items related to hot, cold, and rainy weather (e.g. sunscreen, sunglasses, flip flops; umbrella, raincoat, rubber boots)

Place the objects related to hot weather on the teacher's desk. Ask students, *When do we use these?* and encourage them to notice they are for hot weather. Tell them to close their eyes while you add one or two cold/rainy weather objects. When they open their eyes, ask, *What's wrong?* and invite a student to come up and take away the object(s) related to cold/rainy weather. Repeat this several times, switching the objects and the weather pattern up.

> **Note to teachers**
> This activity introduces the idea of debugging. In coding, a mistake in a coding line is called a *bug*. Identifying them helps solve things that aren't working correctly. Encouraging students to pay close attention and spot mistakes helps them develop debugging skills.

Look and stick. Draw.

Materials and preparation

- Project Book page 17

Help students open their Project Books to page 17. Point to the picture. Ask, *What can you see?* Help them notice that it is a scene at a beach. Elicit the names of the items they can identify. Then ask them to take a closer look. Ask, *What is the weather like? Do we need these things on the beach on a sunny day?* Have students check the items one by one to find the mistakes (raincoat, umbrella, rubber boots). When they have identified the mistakes (bugs), they turn to the stickers page at the back of the book, peel off the bug stickers, and stick them on the incorrect item. Help students with the stickers as needed. Then they draw three more items on the blanket to "correct the mistake".

DIFFERENTIATED INSTRUCTION

BELOW LEVEL
Look and stick. Draw.

Students can draw a check mark or an X in pencil over the incorrect item before placing the stickers to make sure they stick them in the right place.

ABOVE LEVEL
Look and stick. Draw.

Invite students to explain why each of the items is considered "a bug" (because we use them in different weather conditions).

CLOSING

Pick up the clothes. Sing the *Goodbye song*.

Materials and preparation

- A basket
- Audio library – songs
- Clothes for cold and hot weather (flip-flops, boots, coat, swimming suit, shorts, sweater, bikini, skirt, sneakers, T-shirt, scarf)

Spread the clothes around the classroom. Call out each item and have students race to get them. When they have collected all the clothes, have students sit it a circle and put a basket in the middle of the circle. Call out the name of an item — the student with that item throws it in the basket. You should set up expectations of walking safely so as to avoid accidents.
Sing the *Goodbye song* (track 3) and invite students to sing along. Say *goodbye* to them and have them say *goodbye* back to you.

CIRCLE AND COUNT.

PRE-CODING • WHAT HAPPENS TO YOUR BODY WHEN YOU ARE HOT OR COLD? • UNIT 4   19

Learning goals
- Count variables through a game
- Practice using words for clothes

Pre-coding skill
- Variables

Main language content
Clothes: *raincoat, scarf, shorts, sun hat, sweater, swimming suit*
What's your score?

OPENING

Circle time

Materials and preparation
- Puppet
- Visual schedule pictures (hide them around the classroom)

Show the puppet to students and have them greet it with *hello* or *hi*. Remind students of the attention-getter and practice it with them:
T: *Let's take this road!*
S: *It's time to code!*
or
T: *Turn on your fun mode because it's time to…*
S: *Code!*
Hide the visual schedule pictures that refer to today's activities. Tell students to look for them around the classroom. As they find a picture, tell them to hand it to you. Then talk to students about each of the moments of the class.

> **Note to teachers**
> Remind students that they should be quiet and pay attention when you use the attention-getter.

Play *Pictionary*.

Play *Pictionary* with students. Tell them that the theme is clothes. Draw pictures on the board for students to guess the words. Occasionally, you can invite students to draw. Say a word, have them draw it for their classmates to guess. Encourage students to say the words in English.

> **Note to teachers**
> After a student has drawn a picture, ask, *Who is wearing (a T-shirt)? What color is it?* and have the student answer the question.

Pre-coding

ACTIVE LEARNING

Play the *Mime game.*

Tell students that you are the "computer" and they are the "codes", so they have to do what you tell them to do. Give commands related to clothes for hot and cold weather, such as *Put on a hat/raincoat/swimming suit; use an umbrella.* After a few rounds, divide students into groups and invite a student to be the "computer" in their group and give commands to their classmates. Then they can switch roles until each student has had the chance to give a command.

Circle and count.

Materials and preparation

- Pencils
- Printouts of cold, hot, and rainy weather clothes
- Project Book page 19

Help students open their Project Books to page 19. Ask, *What can you see?* Explain that they are going to play a game with the pictures on the page. They have to find the pictures, circle them, and add them to their score. They will have a time limit (around two minutes) to do this. Write the following scoring rules on the board and stick the printouts next to them:

Rules
cold weather clothes – 1 point
hot weather clothes – 2 points
rainy weather clothes – 3 points

Before they start playing the game, check students' understanding by pointing to an umbrella in the picture and asking, *How many points?* Repeat this with different pictures until you are sure that students understand.

Note to teachers
You can change the level of difficulty of this activity by assigning different points to each type of clothing.

Set a time limit and have students play the game on page 19. When time is up, help students add up the points and have them check their score. Find out who got the highest score. Have student point to the pictures they circled and tell you how many points they got for each picture (one, two, or three)

Note to teachers
This activity is linked to the notion of variables. In coding, this is where information is stored, and it is a factor that can change. In this game, the variable is the score (total number of points per picture circled) and students change it by circling more pictures.

DIFFERENTIATED INSTRUCTION

BELOW LEVEL
Circle and count.

Allow students more time to find the pictures on the page.

ABOVE LEVEL
Circle and count.

Materials and preparations

- Buttons

Hand out buttons and have students count out the number of buttons so that it matches their score.

CLOSING

Spin the bottle. Sing the *Goodbye song.*

Materials and preparation

- A bottle
- Audio library – songs

Have students sit in a circle and put the bottle in the middle. Ask them to take turns spinning the bottle. The student the bottle points to when it stops has to say what the weather is like and what clothes they are wearing. Encourage them to be creative! Sing the *Goodbye song* (track 3) and invite students to sing along. Say *goodbye* to them and have them say *goodbye* back to you.

Unit 5 Why is it important to take care of our planet?

PRE-CODING • WHY IS IT IMPORTANT TO TAKE CARE OF OUR PLANET? • UNIT 5 21

Learning goals
- Create a sequence
- Practice using the vocabulary related to helping the environment

Pre-coding skill
- Sequence

Main language content
Helping the planet: *Feed the birds. Take care of plants. Throw trash in the trash can. Turn off the faucet. Turn off the TV.*
What can we do to help the environment?

OPENING

Circle time
Materials and preparation
- Audio library – songs
- Puppet
- Visual schedule pictures

Show the puppet to students and have them greet it with *hello* or *hi*. Sing the *Hello song* (track 2) and have them sing, mime, and dance. Remind students of the attention-getter and practice it with them:
T: *Let's take this road!*
S: *It's time to code!*
or
T: *Turn on your fun mode because it's time to...*
S: *Code!*
Have students sit in a circle. Show them the visual schedule pictures. Ask for volunteers to help you turn them over. Encourage the whole class to say what each picture shows. Choose a class helper of the day and have them order the pictures of the activities as they are mentioned.

> **Note to teachers**
> You can also teach/review the attention-getter *All set? You bet!*

Sing 1, 2, Buckle my shoe.
Materials and preparation
- Audio library – songs (or another song students like)

Sing *1, 2, Buckle my shoe* (track 15) or any other song students like and encourage them to sing along and do the gestures. Pause the song occasionally and encourage students to keep on singing without the music.

24 Pre-coding

ACTIVE LEARNING

Numbers sequence
Materials and preparation
- Squares of paper with the numbers 1 to 50 written on them

Gather students in a circle. Spread the numbers in the middle of the circle and invite students to put them in order, from 1 to 50. Make sure to count the numbers at the end to check that they are correct. You can change the numbers according to students' ability, e.g. 1 to 30, 1 to 70, or 1 to 100.

> **Note to teachers**
> You can do this activity as a whole class or divide students into smaller groups and give each group a sequence of numbers, e.g. 1 to 20, 21 to 40, etc.

Look and number.
Materials and preparation
- Pencils
- Project Book page 21

Help students open their Project Books to page 21. Point to each picture and encourage them to say the actions the children are doing. Ask them to imagine that they are doing these activities at their house. Tell them to number the pictures 1 to 5 according to the order that they would do them.

> **Note to teachers**
> This activity works on sequencing. In coding, the program has to follow an order, or sequence.

Sequence role-play
Materials and preparation
- Project Book page 21

Depending on the size of your class, this activity can be done in pairs, small groups, or as a whole class. A student says the sequence of activities in the Project Book, according to how they numbered them, while the other students act it out in the correct order.

DIFFERENTIATED INSTRUCTION

BELOW LEVEL
Look and number.

Write numbers one to five on the board to help students understand how to number to pictures in order.

ABOVE LEVEL
Look and number.
Materials and preparation
- Crayons or colored pencils
- Sheets of paper

Encourage students to think about other sequences they would do these actions. They can draw them in a separate sheet of paper.

CLOSING

Do the puzzle. Sing the *Goodbye song*.
Materials and preparation
- Audio library – songs
- Jigsaw puzzles

Gather students in a circle. Spread the puzzle pieces on the floor in the middle of the circle and invite students to put the puzzle together. Check quickly they can complete *it*? You can either do one puzzle for the whole group or split students into groups and give them a puzzle each. Sing the *Goodbye song* (track 3) and invite students to sing along. Say *goodbye* to them and have them say *goodbye* back to you.

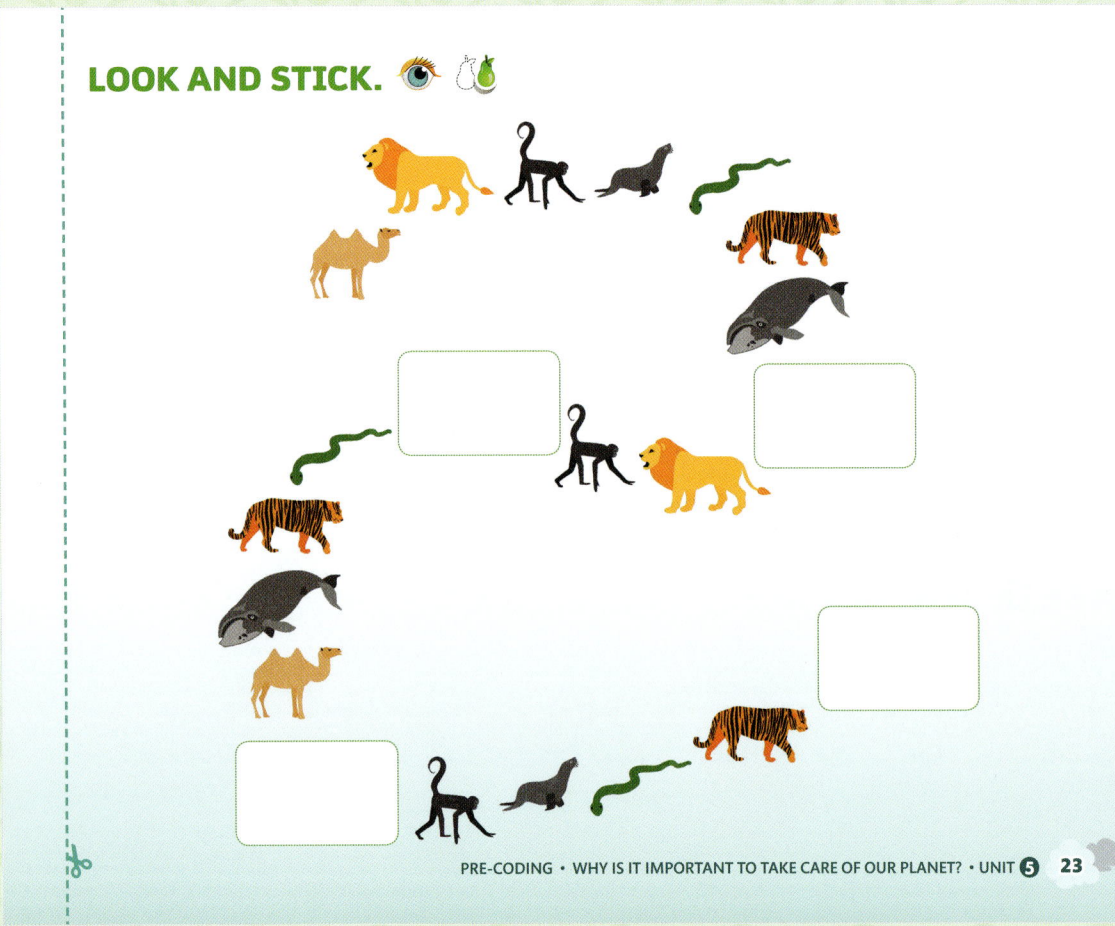

Learning goals
- Recognize a pattern
- Practice using words for animals and their habitats

Pre-coding skill
- Pattern

Main language content
Animals: *camel, fox, lion, monkey, polar bear, seal, snake, tiger, whale*
Habitats: *Arctic, desert, jungle*
Where does it live?

OPENING

Circle time
Materials and preparation
- Puppet
- Visual schedule pictures

Show the puppet to students and have them greet it with *hello* or *hi*. Remind students of the attention-getter and practice it with them:
T: *Let's take this road!*
S: *It's time to code!*
or
T: *Turn on your fun mode because it's time to…*
S: *Code!*
Show students the visual schedule pictures. Ask for volunteers to help you turn them over. Encourage the whole class to say what each picture shows. Ask students to help you select the pictures that show today's schedule as you tell them what they are going to do today.

> **Note to teachers**
> Remind students that they should be quiet and pay attention when you use the attention-getter.

Where does it live?
Materials and preparation
- Pictures of camel, fox, lion, monkey, polar bear, seal, snake, tiger, and whale
- Pictures of the Arctic, the desert, and the jungle.

Tell students that there are three different habitats in the classroom: the Arctic, the desert, and the jungle. Ask them to say what these habitats are like and what animals live there. Assign an area of the classroom to each habitat. Show the printouts of the animals one by one and ask, *Where does it live?* Students move to the correct "habitat" in the classroom.
You should set up expectations of walking safely so as to avoid accidents.

> **Note to teachers**
> Encourage students to walk and make sounds like the animal as they walk, e.g. they jump and make sounds like a monkey as they move over to "jungle".

ACTIVE LEARNING

Make a pattern

Materials and preparation
- Crayons
- Long strips of paper (one per student)

Give each student a strip of paper and ask them to choose two different colored crayons. Have students color squares on the strip of paper using the two colors, making a pattern. If necessary, demonstrate this on the board using different colored markers before students begin. When they have finished, have them read their patterns aloud, e.g. *red, blue, red, red, blue*, etc.

> **Note to teachers**
> This activity helps students get familiar with pattern recognition. When there is a problem with a program or app the coders look for patterns that they have not seen before. If they find these patterns, they will know what is wrong and they will be able to fix it.

Look and stick.

Materials and preparation
- Project Book page 23

Help students open their Project Books to page 23. Point to each picture and ask, *What's it?* Encourage them to say the names of the animals. Have students turn to the stickers page, peel off the stickers, and complete the pattern. Help them with the stickers as needed. Tell them not to worry if they can't spot the pattern straight away. Encourage them to keep looking. When they finish, have them compare in pairs. Encourage them to point to the pictures and say the name of the animal.

Say the habitat

Materials and preparation
- Project Book page 23

Once students have finished identifying the pattern, organize them into pairs and have them say where the animals live. Encourage them to point to each picture, say the name of the animal and its habitat.

DIFFERENTIATED INSTRUCTION

BELOW LEVEL
Look and stick.

Go over the pictures of the animals, one by one, and help students identify what comes next.

ABOVE LEVEL
Look and stick.

Ask students to try to continue the pattern. Ask, *What would come next? And after that?*

CLOSING

Play *Sleeping lions*. Sing the *Goodbye song*.

Materials and preparation
- Audio library – songs

Play *Sleeping lions* with students. All students lie on the floor and pretend to be asleep like lions. Walk around and act like a monkey, trying to make students laugh, move, or wake up. As soon as a student moves, they join you in acting like a monkey and try to make the other students move. If you have a large class, students can pretend to sleep on their seats.
Sing the *Goodbye song* (track 3) and invite students to sing along. Say *goodbye* to them and have them say *goodbye* back to you.

Unit 6 How can you stay healthy?

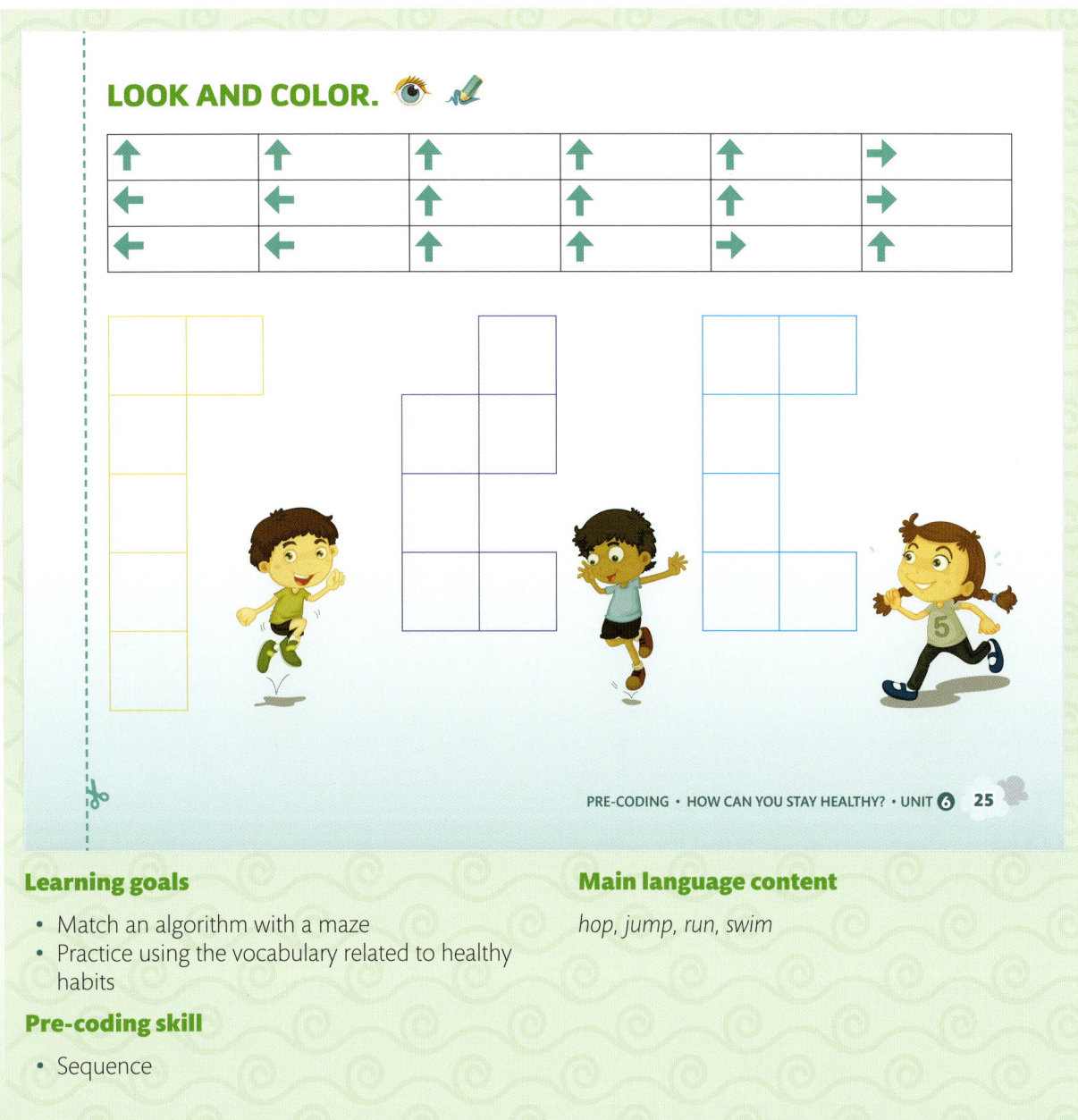

OPENING

Circle time

Materials and preparation
- Audio library – songs
- Puppet
- Visual schedule pictures

Show the puppet to students and have them greet it with *hello* or *hi*. Sing the *Hello song* (track 2) and have them sing, mime, and dance. Remind students of the attention-getter and practice it with them:
T: *Let's take this road!*
S: *It's time to code!*
or
T: *Turn on your fun mode because it's time to…*
S: *Code!*
Have students sit in a circle. Show them the visual schedule pictures. Ask for volunteers to help you turn them over. Encourage the whole class to say what each picture shows. Choose a class helper of the day and have them order the pictures of the activities as they are mentioned.

> **Note to teachers**
> You can also teach/review the attention-getter *All set? You bet!*

Sing *If you are happy and you know it.*

Materials and preparation
- Audio library – songs (or another song students like)

Sing *If you're happy and you know it* (track 11) or any other song students like and encourage them to sing along and do the gestures. Pause the song occasionally and encourage students to keep on singing without the music.

Learning goals
- Match an algorithm with a maze
- Practice using the vocabulary related to healthy habits

Pre-coding skill
- Sequence

Main language content
hop, jump, run, swim

Pre-coding

ACTIVE LEARNING

Circle fun!

Gather students in a large circle and tell them to walk around in the circle. Call out an action (*hop, jump, run, swim*) and have students move around in the circle doing that movement. Alternate between the actions.
You should set up expectations of walking safely so as to avoid accidents.

> **Note to teachers**
> You can invite students randomly to call out one or two actions and have the class to repeat the movements.

How do I get there?

Materials and preparation
- Masking tape (optionally, EVA foam mat - squares of different colors)
- Toy cars (or other vehicles)

On the floor, draw a grid similar to the one below using masking tape. On the board, draw the arrows: →, ↑, ↓, ←. Check students' understanding of them by asking them to stand up, pointing to the arrows, and asking students to move in that direction. Ask students to sit/stand around the grid on the floor. Invite a student to take a toy car and place it at the front of the grid. Ask the student to move the car along the grid, one square at a time. As students do so, point to the arrows on the board and ask them to identify which shows the direction the car is moving in. Draw the arrows on the board until you have drawn the "code" to move along the grid.
Alternatively you can also use EVA foam mat of different colors to create the grid on the floor.

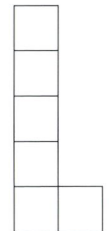

> **Note to teachers**
> In coding, an algorithm is a sequence of instructions for a computer to complete a task. In this activity, students identify the instructions to follow to make the car move along the grid.

Look and color.

Materials and preparation
- Crayons: blue, purple, and yellow
- Project Book page 25

Help students open their Project Books to page 25. Point to each picture showing a child doing an action and ask, *What are they doing?* Tell students that the children want to move along their grids, but they need their help. Students work in pairs to match the instructions with each grid. (First line of arrows with the boy jumping; second line of arrows with the girl walking, and the third line of arrows with the boy hopping). Once they have matched it, they color the instructions in the same color as the grid.

DIFFERENTIATED INSTRUCTION

BELOW LEVEL
Look and color.

Materials and preparation
- Small squares of paper with the arrows on them (at least 11 up arrows, 4 right, and 4 left per student)

Give students small cutout squares with the arrows drawn on them. Students can place the squares on the grid to help them before coloring the page.

ABOVE LEVEL
Look and color.

Students draw an arrow in each square to show the code.

CLOSING

Let's play! Sing the *Goodbye song*.

Materials and preparation
- Audio library – songs
- Masking tape

Mark large versions of the grids in the Project Book on the floor using masking tape. In pairs, students take turns giving each other instructions to hop, run, jump, and swim along the grid.
Sing the *Goodbye song* (track 3) and invite students to sing along. Say *goodbye* to them and have them say *goodbye* back to you.

Unit 6

PRE-CODING • HOW CAN YOU STAY HEALTHY? • UNIT 6   27

Learning goals
- Break down a picture into smaller parts
- Practice using words for food

Pre-coding skill
- Decomposition

Main language content
Food: *cheese, corn, cucumber, lettuce, salad, tomato*

OPENING

Circle time

Materials and preparation
- Puppet
- Visual schedule pictures (hide them around the classroom)

Show the puppet to students and have them greet it with *hello* or *hi*. Remind students of the attention-getter and practice it with them:
T: *Let's take this road!*
S: *It's time to code!*
or
T: *Turn on your fun mode because it's time to…*
S: *Code!*
Hide the visual schedule pictures that refer to today's activities. Tell students to look for them around the classroom. As they find a picture, tell them to hand it to you. Then talk to students about each of the moments of the class.

> **Note to teachers**
> Remind students that they should be quiet and pay attention when you use the attention-getter.

Food mystery bag

Materials and preparation
- A bag filled with different food items (real food or pictures; healthy and unhealthy)

Gather students in a circle and pass the bag around. Students take out an item, show it to the class, and try to name it. Monitor and help as needed. At the end, place all of the food items in the middle of the circle and invite students to separate them into "healthy" and "unhealthy".

ACTIVE LEARNING

Practicing decomposition

Materials and preparation

- Buttons or beads (10 per pair of students)
- Flashcards: numbers 5-10 (one flashcard per pair of students, take copies, if necessary)
- Pencils
- Sheets of paper (at least A4 size) folded into two halves (if you have time, draw a line down the middle of the page)

Divide students into pairs and give each pair a sheet of paper and a number flashcard. Then give them the number of buttons/beads according to the number on their flashcard. Ask them to count the buttons/beads and check they have the right amount. Tell students that they have to put the buttons/beads on each side of their sheet of paper, so that the sum of both sides equals to the number on the flashcard. Check if they have done it correctly. If you have time, hand each pair another flashcard and more buttons/beads so that they can practice it further.

Note to teachers
This activity helps students practice decomposition by breaking down a larger number into a smaller one.

Count and write. Color.

Materials and preparation

- Crayons
- Pencils
- Project Book page 27

Help students open their Project Books to page 27. Point to the picture of the salad and ask, *What's it? Do you like eating it?* Ask them what ingredients they can see in this salad. Students count how many of each ingredient is in the salad and write the number in the box corresponding to that ingredient. Then they color the picture.

DIFFERENTIATED INSTRUCTION

BELOW LEVEL
Count and write. Color.

Students can color the picture first to help them identify the food items to count.

ABOVE LEVEL
Count and write. Color.

Students can add different ingredients to the salad picture, count them, draw them separately, and write the corresponding number.

CLOSING

Play *Dominoes*. Sing the *Goodbye song*.

Materials and preparation

- Audio library – songs
- Dominoes
- Number cards: 1-15

Gather students in a circle and organize them into small groups or pairs. Invite each group/pair to take a domino piece. They count the number of spots on each side and try to match the total with the corresponding number. Then they can share with the class by showing the written number (number card) and the visual representation (domino).
Sing the *Goodbye song* (track 3) and invite students to sing along. Say *goodbye* to them and have them say *goodbye* back to you.

Unit 7 How can you take care of animals?

OPENING

Circle time

Materials and preparation
- Audio library – songs
- Puppet
- Visual schedule pictures

Show the puppet to students and have them greet it with *hello* or *hi*. Sing the *Hello song* (track 2) and have them sing, mime, and dance. Remind students of the attention-getter and practice it with them:
T: *Let's take this road!*
S: *It's time to code!*
or
T: *Turn on your fun mode because it's time to…*
S: *Code!*
Have students sit in a circle. Show them the visual schedule pictures. Ask for volunteers to help you turn them over. Encourage the whole class to say what each picture shows. Choose a class helper of the day and have them order the pictures of the activities as they are mentioned.

> **Note to teachers**
> You can also teach/review the attention-getter *All set? You bet!*

Sing *Mama's taking us to the forest tomorrow.*

Materials and preparation
- Audio library – songs

Sing *Mama's taking us to the forest tomorrow* (track 9) and encourage students to sing along and do the gestures. Pause the song occasionally and encourage students to keep on singing without the music.

Learning goals
- Recognize and follow sequences of numbers
- Talk about wild animals

Pre-coding skill
- Sequence

Main language content
Animals: *cat, crocodile, fish, giraffe, lion, penguin, tiger*
Is it a friendly or a wild animal?

Pre-coding

ACTIVE LEARNING

Wild animals!

Materials and preparation

- A ball
- Audio library – songs (or another song students like)
- Pictures of crocodile, fish, giraffe, lion, penguin, and tiger

Gather students in a circle and show them the pictures one by one, eliciting the names of the animals. Choose one of the pictures to be the "crazy animal". Place the pictures face down in the middle of the circle. Give the ball to a student and play the song *Mama is taking us to the zoo tomorrow* (track 6) or another song that students like. When the music stops, the student who is holding the ball picks up a card and names the animal. If they pick out the "crazy animal", they miss their turn and choose one of their classmates to pick a card and say the word.

Look and draw. Count.

Materials and preparation

- Crayons
- Pencils
- Project Book page 29

Help students open their Project Books to page 29. Ask, *What can you see in the pictures?* Invite them to guess. Tell students to put their pencils on number 1 in the first animal. Ask, *What number do you go to next?* Students join the dots in both pictures. Then they color the pictures and show them to their classmates.

> **Note to teachers**
> Encourage students to count aloud as they read the numbers. Make sure they join them in order to practice sequencing.

Number sequence

Materials and preparation

- Numbers cards: 1-30

Gather students in a circle and scatter the numbers cards in the middle. Invite them to put the numbers in the correct order. Then organize students into small groups and give them five number cards, e.g. 1 to 5, 20 to 25 and ask them to put them in the correct order.

DIFFERENTIATED INSTRUCTION

BELOW LEVEL
Look and draw. Count.

Count the numbers aloud with students to support them as they join the dots.

ABOVE LEVEL
Look and draw. Count.

Once students have completed the drawing, encourage them to point at the numbers and try to count them backwards.

CLOSING

Play *Guess the animal*. Sing the *Goodbye song*.

Materials and preparation

- Audio library – songs
- Pictures of crocodile, fish, giraffe, lion, penguin, tiger, and any other animals that students know

Gather students in a circle. Take a picture of an animal and hold it to your chest, so students can't see it. Describe the animal, e.g. *It's big. It's yellow and brown. It's a wild animal. It eats meat.* Students try to guess the animal before you show them the picture. If you have time and depending on the students' abilities, you can give the pictures of animals to students and encourage them to describe it for their classmates.
Sing the *Goodbye song* (track 3) and invite students to sing along. Say *goodbye* to them and have them say *goodbye* back to you.

OPENING

Circle time

Materials and preparation
- Puppet
- Visual schedule pictures

Show the puppet to students and have them greet it with *hello* or *hi*. Remind students of the attention-getter and practice it with them:
T: *Let's take this road!*
S: *It's time to code!*
or
T: *Turn on your fun mode because it's time to…*
S: *Code!*
Show students the visual schedule pictures. Ask for volunteers to help you turn them over. Encourage the whole class to say what each picture shows. Ask students to help you select the pictures that show today's schedule as you tell them what they are going to do today.

> **Note to teachers**
> Remind students that they should be quiet and pay attention when you use the attention-getter.

What time is it?

Materials and preparation
- Sheets of paper (half of a A4) with numbers 1-12 written on each piece
- Sticky tape

Stick the sheets of paper with the numbers on the board or a wall making a big clock. Call out different times, e.g. *It's (one) o'clock*. Students have to run and touch the right piece of paper as you say the time.
You should set up expectations of walking safely so as to avoid accidents.

Learning goals
- Recognize causes and consequences of actions
- Practice reading the time on the hour

Pre-coding skill
- If-Then

Main language content
What time is it?
It's (six) o'clock.

ACTIVE LEARNING

Time for fun!

Materials and preparation
- A big clock

Gather students in a circle. Show the clock set in different times and ask, *What time is it?* Encourage students to say the time. Then invite students to tell you what they do at each time (use L1 as necessary).

> **Note to teachers**
> All of the activities in this lesson allow students to practice the concept of "if-then" statements. In coding, computers make choices depending on whether something is true or not. In this activity, students think about what they do at certain times, e.g. *If it's twelve o'clock, I eat lunch*.

Look and color.

Materials and preparation
- Crayons or colored pencils
- Project Book page 31

Help students open their Project Books to page 31. Point to the first picture of the computer. Ask, *What time is it?* Then point to the picture of the analog clock and draw students' attention to the different sections in the clock. Count the sections (one to 12) with them. Ask them to identify what section of the clock they need to color in so that it is the same as the time on the computer (seven). Students color the section of the analog clocks according to the time on the digital clock.

> **Note to teachers**
> In this activity, students practice "if-then" thinking because *if* the computer clock shows a time, *then* they color a specific section on the clock picture.

What time is it, Mr. Wolf?

Clear some space in the classroom or go to an outside space. Ask students to stand shoulder to shoulder in a line. Choose one student (or a pair of students if they aren't very confident) to be the "wolf" and stand at the front of the classroom opposite the other students (but not facing them). The students call out, *What time is it Mr. Wolf?* and the "wolf" calls out, *It's (two) o'clock*. The other students step forward that number of times. At any point the "wolf" can call out "lunchtime"— all of the students run away as the "wolf" tries to catch one, who then becomes the "wolf". You should set up expectations of walking safely so as to avoid accidents.

DIFFERENTIATED INSTRUCTION

BELOW LEVEL
Look and color.

Help students by drawing a clock on the board or helping them counting each section.

ABOVE LEVEL
Look and color.

Materials and preparation
- Crayons or colored pencils
- Sheets of paper

Students can draw an along clock (similar to the one in the Project Book) and color one section. Then they show their clocks and say the time, e.g. *It's (three) o'clock*.

CLOSING

Talk about clocks. Sing the *Goodbye song*.

Materials and preparation
- A selection of clocks and watches (e.g. a wall clock, an alarm clock, a watch, a cell phone showing the time, etc.)
- Audio library – songs

Show students the clocks and ask them if they have seen them before. If so, ask them where they have seen them or who uses them.
Sing the *Goodbye song* (track 3) and invite students to sing along. Say *goodbye* to them and have them say *goodbye* back to you.

Unit 8 What is your favorite place in town?

Learning goals
- Recognize mistakes in a picture
- Talk about what people do and where they do it

Pre-coding skill
- Debugging

Main language content

Community workers: *baker, chef, doctor, firefighter, nurse, street cleaner, teacher*
Places in town: *bakery, bank, café, fire station, hospital, restaurant, school*

OPENING

Circle time

Materials and preparation
- Audio library – songs
- Puppet
- Visual schedule pictures

Show the puppet to students and have them greet it with *hello* or *hi*. Remind students of the attention-getter and practice it with them:
T: *Let's take this road!*
S: *It's time to code!*
or
T: *Turn on your fun mode because it's time to…*
S: *Code!*
Have students sit in a circle. Show them the visual schedule pictures. Ask for volunteers to help you turn them over. Encourage the whole class to say what each picture shows. Choose a class helper of the day and have them order the pictures of the activities as they are mentioned.

> **Note to teachers**
> You can also teach/review the attention-getter *All set? You bet!*

Sing *The wheels on the bus*.

Materials and preparation
- Audio library – songs

Sing *The wheels on the bus* (track 10) and encourage students to sing along and do the gestures. Pause the song occasionally and encourage students to keep on singing without the music.

Pre-coding

ACTIVE LEARNING

Act it out!

Materials and preparation

- Flashcards: *baker, chef, doctor, firefighter, teacher*

In the middle of the classroom, line up chairs for about half of the students. Have students stand up. Explain that you will hold up a flashcard and they need to go around the classroom pretending to be the person on the flashcard. When you call out *stop* students need to freeze. The students that do not freeze in time will go sit on the chairs. Then they get to choose the flashcards for their classmates to role-play. When all the seats are taken, the students still standing are the winners, and you can play the game again.

Where do they work?

Materials and preparation

- Flashcards: *baker, chef, doctor, firefighter, teacher*

Gather students in a circle and show the flashcards one by one. Ask them if they can remember how their classmates were acting when they were pretending to do these jobs. Talk with students about the people on the flashcards — what they do and where they work.

What's wrong? Circle and color.

Materials and preparation

- Crayons
- Pencils
- Project Book page 33

Help students open their Project Books to page 33. Focus students' attention on the picture. Elicit the names of the places. Then ask them to take a close look. Ask them if the community workers all doing the right job. Students find the mistakes and circle them. Then they color the community workers in the picture.

DIFFERENTIATED INSTRUCTION

BELOW LEVEL
What's wrong? Circle and color.

Remind students to try to color in the lines when they color the picture — some students may struggle with this due to the small size.

ABOVE LEVEL
What's wrong? Circle and color.

Materials and preparation

- Colored pencils
- Scissors (optional)
- Sheets of paper

Students can draw the community workers in the right place, doing the right job. Then they can cut out their drawings and place them on the corresponding part of the picture in their Project Books to "correct" it.

CLOSING

Play *Guess the community worker*. Sing the *Goodbye song*.

Materials and preparation

- Audio library – songs
- Flashcards: *baker, chef, doctor, firefighter, teacher*

Choose a pair of students and ask them to take a flashcard. One student pretends to interview the other one about their job (use L1 as necessary) and the other students try to guess the job.
Sing the *Goodbye song* (track 3) and invite students to sing along. Say *goodbye* to them and have them say *goodbye* back to you.

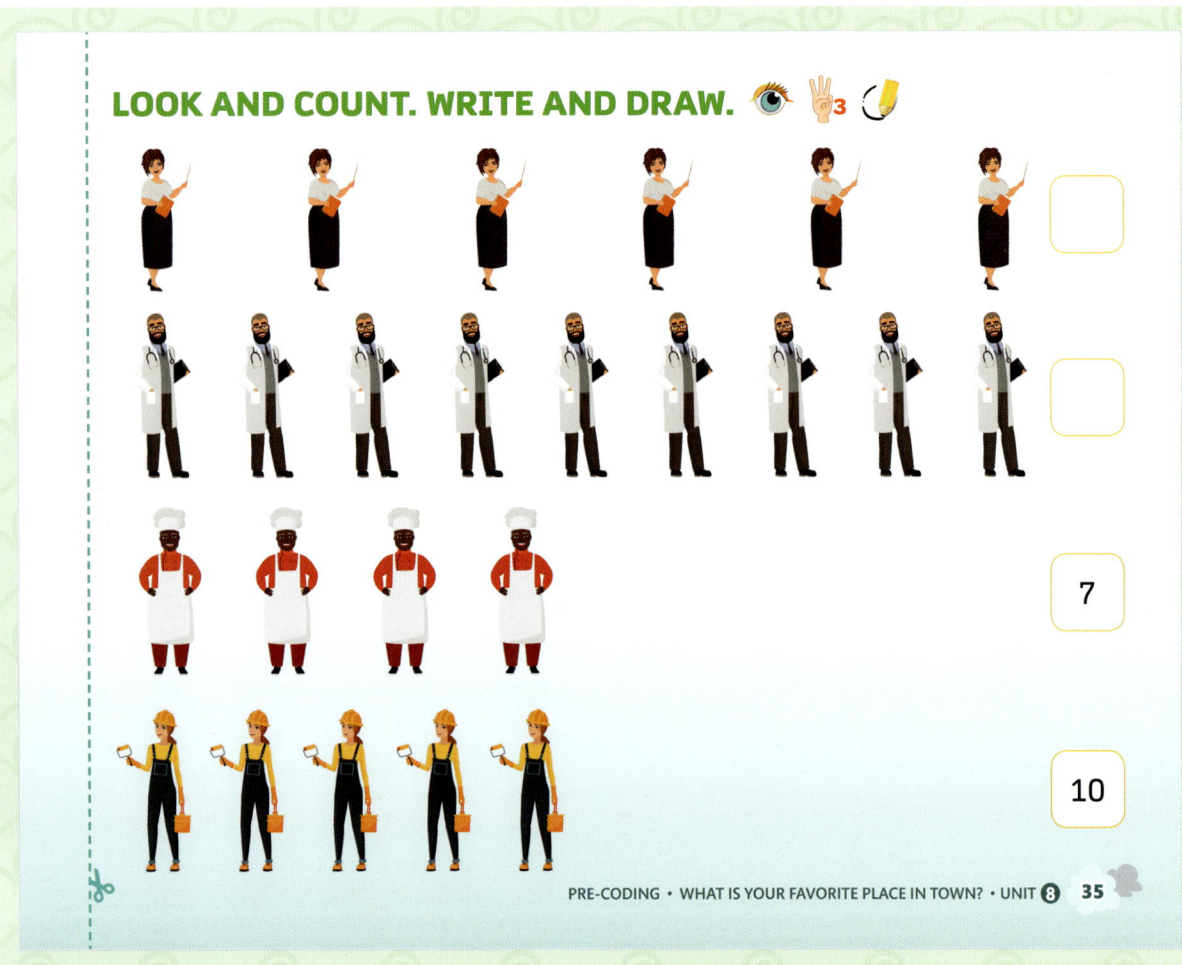

Learning goals
- Identify how many times something needs to be done to get a result
- Talk about what people do and where they do it

Pre-coding skill
- Looping

Main language content
- Community workers: *chef, construction worker, doctor, teacher*

OPENING

Circle time

Materials and preparation
- Puppet
- Visual schedule pictures (hide them around the classroom)

Show the puppet to students and have them greet it with *hello* or *hi*. Remind students of the attention-getter and practice it with them:
T: *Let's take this road!*
S: *It's time to code!*
or
T: *Turn on your fun mode because it's time to…*
S: *Code!*
Hide the visual schedule pictures that refer to today's activities. Tell students to look for them around the classroom. As they find a picture, tell them to hand it to you. Then talk to students about each of the moments of the class.

> **Note to teachers**
> Remind students that they should be quiet and pay attention when you use the attention-getter.

Play *I spy.*

Gather students in a circle and ask them to close their eyes. Tell them to imagine they are standing in the middle of a town. Ask them what they see. Invite students to raise their hands and then call on these students to say what they can see using "I spy", e.g. *I spy a bakery!* If necessary, talk about places in town with students before the activity to check their understanding.

ACTIVE LEARNING

How many times?

Materials and preparation
- Different toys (if possible, one per student)

Place some toys on one side of the classroom, opposite students. Invite a student to stand up and ask the other students to choose an action, e.g. *hop, jump*. Ask the students to guess how many times their classmate has to hop/jump before they get to the toys. Then the student moves toward the toys as the other students count. Ask them if they guessed it correctly. The student who was moving takes a toy and runs back. Repeat this with other students until there are no toys left. You should set up expectations of walking safely so as to avoid accidents.

> **Note to teachers**
> This lesson works on the notion of looping. In coding, a loop is an algorithm (set of instructions) that repeats a certain number until a specific result is achieved.

Look and count. Write and draw.

Materials and preparation
- Pencils
- Project Book page 35

Help students open their Project Books to page 35. Have them observe the page. Elicit the names of the community workers they already know and what they do. Teach them the name of community workers they don't know by pointing to the picture and saying the word. For the first two lines, students count the number of times the community worker do their job and then write the number. For the final two lines, they look at the number, count how many pictures are already on the page, and draw the missing pictures.

> **Note to teachers**
> This activity practices looping because students count how many times an action is repeated until the community worker can do something.

Act it out

Materials and preparation
- Project Book page 35

Pair students up and ask them to take turns role playing the community workers shown in the Project Book. Make sure they repeat the actions the same amount of times.

DIFFERENTIATED INSTRUCTION

BELOW LEVEL
Look and count. Write and draw.

Materials and preparation
- Buttons or beads

For the final two lines, give students buttons or beads. They place them on page 35 of their Project Books to represent the numbers to help them work out how many pictures to draw.

ABOVE LEVEL
Look and count. Write and draw.
- Crayons or colored pencils
- Sheets of paper

Students can draw another community worker and the loop.

CLOSING

Role-play being community workers. Sing the *Goodbye song*.

Materials and preparation
- Audio library – songs
- Props related to community workers (optional).

Divide students into groups and have each group decide on a role-play related to the community workers and the places in town. Give them props if you have these available. Allow students time to organize themselves and present to their classmates.
Sing the *Goodbye song* (track 3) and invite students to sing along. Say *goodbye* to them and have them say *goodbye* back to you.

Notes

Notes

Notes

Notes

Notes

Notes

Notes

Notes

Notes